ALL ABOUT
GARDEN WILDLIFE

ALL ABOUT GARDEN WILDLIFE

David Chandler

NEW HOLLAND

First published in 2008 by New Holland Publishers (UK) Ltd
London • Cape Town • Sydney • Auckland

www.newhollandpublishers.com

Garfield House, 86-88 Edgware Road, London W2 2EA, United Kingdom
80 McKenzie Street, Cape Town 8001, South Africa
Unit 1, 66 Gibbes Street, Chatswood, New South Wales, Australia 2067
218 Lake Road, Northcote, Auckland, New Zealand

ISBN 978 1 84773 052 7

Senior Editor: Krystyna Mayer
Design: Fetherstonhaugh (www.fetherstonhaugh.com)
Production: Melanie Dowland
Editorial Consultant: James Parry
Editorial Direction: Rosemary Wilkinson

Reproduction by Modern Age Repro House Ltd, Hong Kong
Printed and bound in Malaysia by Time Offset (M) SDN Bhd

CONTENTS

THE VARIETY OF GARDEN WILDLIFE

Going wild in the garden

This book is all about garden wildlife. When you think about great places to watch wildlife, you probably don't think of your garden! You might think of lions, Wildebeest and antelopes in Africa, colourful birds and beautiful butterflies in tropical forests, penguins and Killer Whales in Antarctica. Here in the UK, seabird colonies might come to mind with comical Puffins, diving Gannets and penguin-like Razorbills and Guillemots. Or maybe you'd prefer a warm, sunny day watching butterflies and dragonflies by a beautiful lake or river.

But hang on a minute. You don't actually have to go far to see wildlife – it's never far away. If you've got a garden, you already have your very own study area and a great place to make your own wildlife discoveries. It may not have any lions, but there are some awesome predators there and plenty of species that do things that will surprise you! Garden wildlife isn't just birds, bees and butterflies – there are more animals out there than you realize.

Birds may be the most obvious visitors to your garden, though, especially if you put out food for them. Starlings, House Sparrows, Blackbirds, Robins, pigeons, tits and finches are often seen in gardens. If you're lucky you might have House Martins nesting under the edge of your roof, or a Sparrowhawk hunting in the neighbourhood – it might even stop in your garden to pluck its next meal!

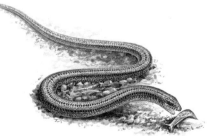

You don't have to go to Africa to see mammals. Your house might be a roost site for the Common Pipistrelle, a tiny bat. If it isn't, you could put up a bat box to encourage these nocturnal creatures. Grey Squirrels might raid your birdfeeders, and in some areas the smaller, cuter-looking Red Squirrel visits gardens. Hedgehogs are often seen in gardens, and small mammals such as mice, voles and shrews could be there too, but may be hard to see. Depending on where you live and what your garden's like, there could be big mammals too – a Red Fox or even a Badger.

Frogs, toads and newts breed in garden ponds, and a Grass Snake might hunt there – watch out frogs! Open compost heaps are good for Grass Snakes too, and are one place where you might see a Slow Worm, a lizard with no legs that looks a bit like a snake.

That's just the vertebrates (the animals with backbones). There are even more invertebrates (animals without backbones) that make a living in gardens. Butterflies can be easy to see. Red Admirals, Peacocks and Small Tortoiseshells bring great colours into a garden. There are moths that fly during the day, and hundreds of moth species that fly at night. Some of them are very impressive – take a look at the Garden Tiger on page 24.

Dragonflies bring colour too. You don't need a pond to see them – but it does help. Aphids and bees find food in plants, and the aphids are food for ladybirds. Look in long grass for grasshoppers. Turn over logs and rubble to search for many-legged centipedes and millipedes, woodlice (relatives of lobsters!) and fierce predatory beetles. Check out hoverflies that pretend to be bees or wasps to protect themselves. Spiders, worms, slugs, snails, ants... many, many creatures are found just outside your door. **Enjoy!**

WHY GARDENS ARE IMPORTANT

In Britain today, more than ever, gardens are important places for wildlife. The countryside is under pressure like never before. We live in a small country with lots of people. We need land for houses and to grow food, and we're still building new roads. In the countryside there is less woodland than there used to be and fewer ponds. Many miles of hedgerow have been removed and land may be worked very hard to produce as much food as possible. This can make it tough for wildlife, but gardens can help, especially if they are looked after in a wildlife-friendly way.

Believe it or not, if you stuck all the gardens in Britain together, they would cover more land than all of the country's nature reserves put together. If we use our gardens well, they can provide food and shelter for wildlife that's having a hard time in the countryside.

A garden doesn't need to be big to make a difference. Whatever the size of your garden it's probably next to other gardens or maybe to some farmland or woodland. Imagine how that would look to a bird flying overhead – your garden would be part of something much bigger. It might even be part of a 'green corridor' connecting farmland to woodland. It's a small chunk of a much bigger area of wildlife habitat.

Not all gardens are the same. Your garden will probably be very different from the gardens of your neighbours, and there will be variety within it too. It will probably contain a number of different habitats, which will

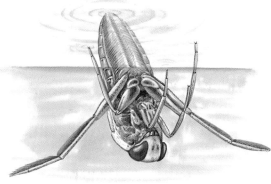

attract different creatures. A lawn could be loaded with earthworms, making it a great feeding area for Blackbirds. There could be crane-fly larvae (leatherjackets) under the lawn – Starlings like to eat these. The flowers could attract nectar-feeding bees, butterflies and moths. Ladybirds might eat the aphids in the vegetable patch. You might have trees and bushes, perhaps a pond with snails, dragonflies, water boatmen and pond skaters, a compost heap, a shed and maybe a pile of logs or stones. Variety is good – the more varied your garden is, the more creatures it is likely to attract.

If you want some ideas to help you make your garden better for wildlife, take a look at pages 12–13. Gardens really can make a difference. Garden ponds have become very important for Common Frogs, and many records of Stag Beetles are now from British gardens. Goldfinches were getting rarer, but providing seed for them in garden birdfeeders may have played a part in helping their numbers to go up again.

One of the best things about watching garden wildlife is that it is right on your doorstep. You can go there often and see how it changes through the year. You can even watch it from inside the house! Whatever its size, a garden can be a great place to enjoy wildlife – so what are you waiting for?

SOME GARDEN WILDLIFE-WATCHING TIPS

If you use your eyes and ears, take your time and look carefully, you could find all sorts of creatures that you didn't know were there. Here are some things you can do to enjoy your garden's wildlife.

Enjoy the dawn chorus May is a good time to listen to what can be an amazing blast of early-morning birdsong. You don't even need to get out of bed! Just wake up early (about 4–4.30 a.m.), open a window, lie back and enjoy.

Turn over logs, rocks or rubble and see what you can find. These spots can be good habitats for centipedes, millipedes, woodlice, beetles and maybe even a newt or toad.

Explore your compost heap Enclosed compost heaps can be great for minibeasts. Open heaps sometimes provide a home for Grass Snakes.

Get a spade and do some digging You might be surprised at the creatures you find living in the soil. Look for worms, millipedes, centipedes and insect larvae. Birds such as Robins and Blackbirds quickly spot that there's an easy meal to be had and may come very close.

Get an old white sheet and put it on the ground under the branch of a tree or bush. Give the branch a shake and see what lands on the sheet. When you have finished looking at the creatures you find, shake the sheet very gently close to the ground to allow them to move off it without being injured.

Use the garden shed as a hide to watch wildlife from. Or make your own wildlife-watching hide.

Watch for bats as you sit outside while the sun goes down.

Leave an outside light on to attract moths and other night-flying insects. If you're allowed, leave the bathroom light on and the window open and enjoy the 'catch' in the morning.

If you think you have hedgehogs in your garden (maybe you've seen some black, shiny droppings with bits of insects in them), come out at night with a torch and see what you can find. Put some red see-through plastic over the lens of the torch. The red light that this produces is less likely to disturb wildlife than a white light would.

Always respect the animals that you find in your garden. Don't handle them any more than you need to, and put them back where you found them as soon as you can. Don't keep them as pets – they may live in your garden, but they are wild animals. Take care to put any logs or rocks back where you found them – that's someone's home you've been moving! Make sure a grown-up knows what you're doing – you might need their help and you may get them interested too.

ATTRACTING WILDLIFE TO YOUR GARDEN

Once you get the wildlife bug, you will probably want
to attract even more creatures into your garden.
There are three things that animals will come to
your garden for – food, water and shelter. Here
are some of the ways in which you can
provide these.

Feed the birds You can use food scraps
from the house (try small bits of bread,
cheese, apple or baked, mashed or boiled
potatoes), or buy special birdseed and
feeders. If you buy birdseed, try to buy
seed that's recommended by a bird
conservation organization.

Provide water A wildlife pond, even a small
one, is a great addition to a wildlife garden. If you can't have a pond, find a
shallow dish and put water in it for birds to drink from and bathe in.
Change the water regularly.

Put up some boxes Put up nest boxes for birds
and maybe some bat boxes. You can also buy or
make boxes for butterflies, ladybirds, hedgehogs
and other species.

Create some minibeast habitats Make a pile of
logs, stones or sticks. Let an area of grass grow
long. Tie some twigs into a bundle and put them
in the fork of a tree, or tuck them away on the
ground somewhere.

Plant for wildlife The fruits of the rowan, crab
apple, holly, hawthorn, cotoneaster and
pyracantha are good bird food. Buddleia and
lavender will attract lots of butterflies. Plant
sunflowers and watch Greenfinches eat the
seeds. Ivy is great – insects feed on its nectar

and use it for hibernation, and birds eat the berries and build nests in it. Take care with garden berries – some are poisonous to people. If there is a spare patch in your garden, allow nettles to grow wild in it – many butterflies, like the beautiful Red Admiral, Small Tortoiseshell and Peacock, love them!

Using this book

This book includes a range of invertebrates and vertebrates that you can find in gardens. We couldn't fit everything in – there are just so many species that can be seen in gardens! Those that are included will give you an idea of what you might see and help you to get to know some of the major groups of animals that are seen in gardens. Some of the animals that you see will be in this book, but you will find others that aren't.

That's enough reading. Time to get out and find some wildlife!

COMMON EARTHWORM
LUMBRICUS TERRESTRIS

Did you know?

If a worm is cut in two you don't get two worms – you will probably get two bits of dead worm, although one part may survive.

When to see All year round.

Where to see Common across Britain and in continental Europe in most types of soil. Dig in the garden and you will probably find earthworms. There are around ten species in gardens – this one is common, and is the biggest British species.

What to look for A pink to brownish worm with pointed front end and blunt rear. An 'adult' has a saddle on its body, which makes a slimy bag for its eggs. It has 110–160 segments, each with eight bristles in pairs, on its 'belly'. These help it to move. There are no eyes, but earthworms are sensitive to light and try to stay in dark places. They are 'hermaphrodite', which means that each one is both male and female. 90–300 mm long.

What they eat Small bits of dead leaves and other organic material, found in the soil or on the surface.

Worms swallow soil as they tunnel through it. Some worms leave it at the surface as a worm cast.

When to see Any time of year, although it hibernates (look for 'sealed-up' shells). It tends to hide away during the day. After rain or at night are good times to look for it.

Where to see Common across Europe, including Britain, in woods, fields, gardens and parks. You can find it under logs, bricks and stones, and on walls behind plants.

What to look for A big snail. The shell is normally brown with dark markings, and can be up to 40 mm across. The body is dark grey. There are four tentacles and white lips. This is one of 80 British snail species.

What they eat Many different types of plant near the ground, especially hostas.

Did you know?

Some snail species are eaten by people, and this is one of them. In France this snail is regarded as a tasty treat!

LARGE BLACK SLUG

ARION ATER

One of about 20 British slug species, the Large Black Slug is often black, but can be brown, grey, off-white and even orange. To protect itself from predators, it changes shape and becomes a swaying, shrivelled 'half-ball'. Up to about 150 mm long.

COMMON FIELD GRASSHOPPER
CHORTHIPPUS BRUNNEUS

When to see Sunny days between June and October.

Where to see Common in Britain and northern and central continental Europe. Likes dry grassy areas, often with bare patches of earth.

What to look for It can be black, purple or different shades of green or brown. The narrow wings are longer than the abdomen, and it is hairy under the thorax. Listen for its song: a short chirp repeated 6–10 times, with roughly 2-second intervals. This is one of Britain's 30 grasshopper and cricket species. About 20 mm long.

What they eat Grass.

Did you know?
If grasshoppers are caught by a predator they will kick with their strong hind legs and throw up!

OAK BUSH CRICKET

MECONEMA THALASSINUM

This cricket lives in trees including oak and apple, but is most likely to be seen around lights that are left on after dark. Male Oak Bush Crickets don't sing to attract females – they drum! The male uses a leaf as a drum and his back legs as drumsticks. The sound is very quiet, though – you are not likely to hear it. About 11–16 mm long.

HOUSE CRICKET
ACHETA DOMESTICUS

Did you know?
A scientist once counted a House Cricket's chirps. In four hours there were 42,000!

When to see At any time of year. It is mostly active at night.

Where to see Common in Britain and on most of the Continent. Lives in houses, gardens and rubbish dumps. Likes warm spots.

What to look for It's normally brown with black markings. It has impressive back legs and long antennae. Its chirping, bird-like song can be heard from late evening and into the night. 15–20 mm long.

What they eat Love rotting plants. Also invertebrates and dead animals. Sometimes, the parents eat their children!

COMMON EARWIG
FORFICULA AURICULARIA

When to see At any time of year. It is active at night, hiding under rocks, logs and in other nooks and crannies during the day.

Where to see Common in Britain and on the Continent. Found in many different habitats, including gardens.

What to look for A long brown insect. Its abdomen is darker than the rest of its body. The males and females have pincers at the end of the abdomen. Up to 20 mm long.

What they eat Rotting plants and animals, fruit, flowers and invertebrates.

Did you know?
Male earwigs use their pincers to fight other males and to warn off hedgehogs and shrews that might eat them.

COMMON GREEN SHIELD BUG
PALOMENA PRASINA

When to see All year except winter. Look for the larvae in summer – they look like small wingless adults.

Where to see In gardens, woods, hedgerows and grassy areas across Britain and much of the Continent.

What to look for Shield-shaped green bug 10–15 mm long, with brown wingtips visible over the rear of the abdomen. In the autumn it turns brown and hibernates.

What they eat Feeds on plants – hazel is a favourite.

Did you know?
This beast is also known as the Green Stink Bug because of the stinky chemicals it leaves on plants.

COMMON POND SKATER
GERRIS LACUSTRIS

When to see April to October. The adults hibernate in winter.

Where to see Common on ponds, lakes and slow-moving rivers across Britain and the Continent.

What to look for Small brown-black insect skating over the water's surface. It uses its middle legs to move forwards, back legs to steer and front legs to grab insects. 10 mm long.

What they eat It senses the vibrations made by an insect that has fallen into the water and 'paddles' to its next meal.

Did you know?
Pond skaters have water-repellent hairs. These help them to walk on water and keep them dry when they dive.

COMMON FROGHOPPER
PHILAENUS SPUMARIUS

When to see June to October.

Where to see On many different plants in gardens and other habitats in Britain and on the Continent.

What to look for From above, the adults are meant to look a bit like frogs – and they do jump very well! Most are brownish, but colours vary. Look for 'cuckoo-spit' (a white frothy substance) on plants. The larvae make this for protection from predators and drying out. About 6 mm long.

What they eat Plant sap.

Did you know?
Cuckoo spit may sound like a safe place for a larva – but some solitary wasps have worked out that there could be food inside.

GREEN LACEWING
CHRYSOPA PALLENS

When to see May to August, mostly at night.

Where to see Common in most of Europe. Found anywhere with lots of plants, including gardens and woods. It is attracted to lights at night and will come into houses.

What to look for Delicate green insect with big lacy wings, long antennae and golden eyes. When resting, the wings are held like a tent over the body. One of 18 species of lacewing found in Britain – two of which are very similar to this one. About 20 mm long.

What they eat Aphids.

Did you know?
Gardeners should like Green Lacewings because they eat lots of aphids, which can be a garden pest.

SMALL WHITE
PIERIS RAPAE

When to see
March to October.

Where to see
Common across Europe, including most of Britain. Found in gardens and many other habitats. Look for them 'nectaring' on white flowers.

What to look for A mostly white or off-white butterfly. It has two or more generations a year. The upper surface of the front wings has greyish tips in the first generation, blacker tips in the second generation. The female has two black spots on each front wing, while the male has one or none. The second generation is normally bigger, with darker markings than the first. Females have darker markings than males. The lower surface of the back wings is yellow. Wingspan 38–57 mm.

What they eat Adults feed on many flowers. Caterpillar food includes cabbages and similar crops, nasturtiums and garlic mustard.

Did you know?
Every year, lots of Small Whites fly across the sea from mainland Europe, boosting the numbers in Britain.

Small White female

LARGE WHITE
PIERIS BRASSICAE
Usually bigger than Small White, and has bigger and darker markings on wing tips.

GREEN-VEINED WHITE
PIERIS NAPI
Has green scales along veins on lower surfaces of back wings.

Both these butterflies are similar to the Small White, so don't confuse them!

Green-veined White male

PEACOCK
INACHIS IO

When to see Virtually all year round except part of June and July. Hibernates in winter.

Where to see Common in most of Britain and on the Continent.

What to look for An easy butterfly to identify, with impressive eye-spots – one on each wing. Wingspan 63–75 mm.

What they eat Nectar from many garden flowers, including buddleia. Caterpillars eat common nettle.

Did you know?
To scare off predators, Peacocks don't just flash their eye-spots. They can hiss too, a noise they make with their wings!

RED ADMIRAL
VANESSA ATALANTA

When to see Mostly May to November.

Where to see Common in most of Europe, including Britain.

What to look for A stunning insect! Look for the black, white and orange-red pattern on the upper wings. Wingspan 64–78 mm.

What they eat A range of flowers, including buddleia, sedum and ivy. Also rotting fruit. Caterpillars eat common nettle.

Did you know?
Nearly all of 'our' Red Admirals migrate from southern Europe. Some migrate south later in the year, and a few may attempt hibernation. As the climate changes, more of these individuals may survive the winter.

SMALL TORTOISESHELL
AGLAIS URTICAE

Did you know?

The weather affects the colour of Small Tortoiseshells. The warmer it is, the brighter they are.

Common nettle is a favourite caterpillar food.

When to see Some come out of hibernation and fly in March, April or earlier. 'New' butterflies are present from May until October. Autumn is a particularly good time to see them. They hibernate from July.

Where to see Common in most of Britain and other parts of Europe in many habitats.

What to look for An easily identified butterfly, but sometimes wrongly called a Red Admiral. Look for blue markings near wing edges and white mark near front wing tips. Most females are larger than males. Wingspan 45–62 mm.

What they eat Another butterfly that loves buddleia! Also likes dandelion, marigold and other garden flowers. Caterpillars eat common nettle.

SMALL MAGPIE
EURRHYPARA HORTULATA

When to see June to August.

Where to see Common in southern Britain in hedgerows and field edges and on wasteland. It is attracted to light. Found in much of Europe.

What to look for Wings are off-white with black and grey edges and other black markings. Body is yellow with black markings. Wingspan 24–28 mm.

What they eat Look for them on stinging nettles – they are a favourite food of Small Magpie caterpillars.

Did you know?
This is a moth that migrates. It's been spotted on a lightship over 50 km out at sea!

SILVER Y
AUTOGRAPHA GAMMA

When to see Mostly May to September, day or night.

Where to see Common across Europe. Found in many habitats, including gardens. Attracted to light.

What to look for Size and colour are variable. Front wings are dappled with grey and brown, with a 'silver Y' mark and sometimes a hint of purple. Wingspan 40–45 mm.

What they eat Often feeds on garden flowers, including buddleia. Caterpillar food includes common nettle, clovers, cabbages and lettuce.

Did you know?
In spring Silver Ys migrate to Britain from southern Europe, where it's warm enough for them to fly in the winter too.

LARGE YELLOW UNDERWING
NOCTUA PRONUBA

When to see June to November. Active at night.

Where to see Common in many habitats in Europe, including gardens.

What to look for Fairly large moth with wingspan of around 60 mm. Front wings are long and thin. Colour and markings vary. There's always a black dot at the front just in from the wingtip. Back wings are orange-yellow with a black strip near edge and no other markings.

What they eat Caterpillars eat lots of different plants, including grasses, docks and cabbages.

Did you know?
When it flies, a predator follows the colour – but when it lands and closes its wings, the colour disappears.

GARDEN TIGER
ARCTICA CAJA

When to see July to August. Active at night.

Where to see Common in much of Britain, in woods, parks, sand dunes and gardens. Attracted to light. Found throughout continental Europe.

What to look for It's an unmistakeable stunner. Markings vary, but front wings are white and brown, and back wings are orange with blue-black blobs. Wingspan 45–70 mm.

What they eat Caterpillars eat many plants, including docks, common nettle and heather.

Did you know?
Garden Tiger caterpillars are often called 'woolly bears'. Look for them on sunny days, eating nettles perhaps, or sunbathing!

COMMON or SEPTEMBER CRANE FLY

TIPULA PALUDOSA

When to see Any time of year, although it is most common in autumn. Adults are most active at night.

Where to see Common in gardens and on grasslands across Britain. They will come inside houses.

What to look for This is *the* Daddy Long Legs, although other crane flies look similar. It has long legs (which come off easily, so take care if you have to handle one), and one pair of wings. The second pair of wings is reduced to 'halteres', which help it to balance in flight. The wings are brownish with a brown line along the front edge. The female's abdomen ends in a point – this is used for egg laying. Around 25 mm long.

What they eat The adults hardly eat at all, although they might take a bit of nectar. The larvae eat grass roots.

Did you know?

The adults are completely harmless, but the larvae (called leatherjackets) live in the soil and can damage crops.

BLUEBOTTLE
CALLIPHORA VOMITORIA

When to see All year round.

Where to see Common across Britain and continental Europe, around houses, gardens, woods and hedgerows. Look for them sunning themselves on walls. Females lay eggs in fish, meat and animal wounds. Males can be seen on flowers, feeding on nectar.

What to look for Hairy insect with shiny blue bands on the abdomen, black legs and black patches under brownish eyes. About 10 mm long.

What they eat Food includes dead animals, dung and nectar.

Did you know?

To feed, Bluebottles dribble on their food. Their saliva breaks down the food and then they slurp it up!

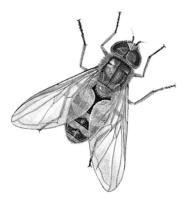

HOVERFLY

SYRPHUS RIBESII

This is one of about 270 British hoverfly species. It hovers and darts around in the air. Look for it drinking nectar from a flower or hovering near flowers. The larvae eat aphids, so they're a gardeners' friend. A hoverfly may look like a wasp, but it's just pretending – it doesn't sting. Its warning colours are a trick, but they still protect the hoverfly from animals that might eat it! About 10 mm long.

SMALL BLACK ANT
LASIUS NIGER

Did you know?

The flying ants that you see in mid-summer are males and queens intent on mating. When the queen has mated she breaks off her wings. She may wait until the following spring before starting a new colony.

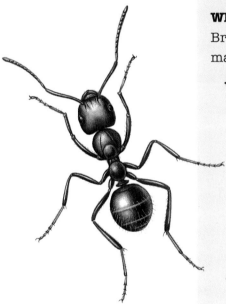

When to see Lives in colonies of thousands that survive from year to year. Winged forms (flying ants) appear on warm days in July or August. Workers (which are wingless) are seen at other times too.

Where to see Common across Britain and continental Europe in many habitats, including gardens.

What to look for The dark-coloured (dark brown or black) garden ant. Workers are about 5 mm long.

What they eat Plant and animal material, including honeydew, small insects and sugary foods. Honeydew is a sweet secretion made by aphids that the ants 'farm'.

RED ANT

MYRMICA RUBRA

The 'red' ant that is seen in gardens. It's not really red – workers and queens are more of a gingery colour, and males are dark brown. Workers can sting, but will only do so if they think you're a serious threat. Most of the Red Ants you see are workers. They are 4 mm long. Queens and males are bigger – they can be 10 mm long.

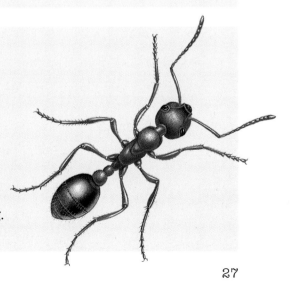

HORNTAIL or WOOD WASP
UROCERUS GIGAS

When to see May to October. Most active on sunny days.

Where to see Common across Britain. Found in pine forests, but also where new houses are being built.

What to look for A large, scary-looking insect – especially the female! The female's 'tail' is in fact a tool for egg-laying (an ovipositor). Horntails don't sting. Females can be 44 mm long. Males are smaller.

What they eat Adults eat pollen. Larvae eat fungi.

Did you know?

The female uses her ovipositor to drill up to 10 mm into wood to lay her eggs. Adults emerge two or three years later.

ICHNEUMON FLY
NETELIA TESTACEA

When to see Summer nights.

Where to see Common across Britain and Ireland in areas with plenty of vegetation.

What to look for An orange insect with long legs and antennae. This is one of about 4,000 species of European ichneumon fly! About 20 mm long.

What they eat Nectar and honeydew.

Did you know?

It lays its eggs on the outsides of moth caterpillars. The eggs hatch, and the larvae gradually eat the caterpillar.

COMMON WASP
VESPULA VULGARIS

When to see Late spring to autumn.

Where to see Common across Britain and continental Europe in many habitats, including gardens.

What to look for Black and yellow abdomen, and black 'anchor' on the front of the face. There are yellow stripes and four yellow spots on the thorax. Most of the wasps you see are workers. They are about 10 mm long. The queens are larger. The males don't appear until late in the season.

What they eat Nectar, fruit and other sugary foods. The larvae eat mainly insects.

Did you know?
The workers and males die in autumn. Only the queens make it through winter, and then start new colonies the following spring.

GERMAN WASP

VESPULA GERMANICA
Another garden wasp. Look for three black dots on the face to tell it from the Common Wasp.

HONEY BEE
APIS MELLIFERA

When to see Spring to autumn.

Where to see Common across Britain and continental Europe. Wild colonies normally nest in holes in trees. Honey Bees are also kept by beekeepers in hives.

What to look for The colours vary, but it is typically brown and hairy, with black and brown striped abdomen. The workers are about 10 mm long. The drones and queens are bigger. A colony can contain 50,000 bees, including a queen, lots of workers (sterile females) and drones (males).

What they eat Nectar and pollen.

Large eyes help a bee to find its colony and recognize flowers for food. Mouthparts are used to spoon up flowers' nectar.

Did you know?
The combs in a Honey Bee nest are vertical. Those in a wasp's nest are horizontal. Honey Bees are very special insects. They are important flower pollinators, and they also make honey!

When to see Late April to October. Most active between June and August.

Where to see Found in Britain and on the Continent in many habitats, including gardens.

What to look for Fairly large, long-haired bumblebee. Look for white tail, and yellow at front of thorax, back of thorax and front of abdomen. Pollen collects on its 'fur' while it is nectaring. This is 'combed' into pollen baskets on its back legs. 20–25 mm long.

What they eat Visits flowers including cowslips, honeysuckle and foxgloves for nectar. Also eats pollen.

CUCKOO BEE

BOMBUS BARBUTELLUS

Cuckoo bees are related to bumblebees. They survive by gatecrashing a bumblebee nest and laying their eggs there, which the bumblebees look after. Cuckoo bees normally look like their bumblebee victims, so they're not easy to spot.

Did you know?

The Garden Bumblebee has a very long tongue – about 13.5 mm. This allows it to get nectar from deeper flowers than is possible for other bumblebees.

VIOLET GROUND BEETLE
CARABUS VIOLACEUS

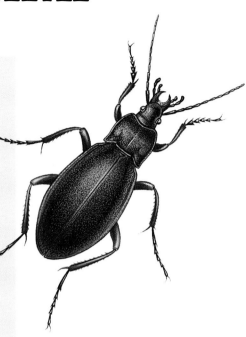

When to see June to August are especially good for seeing adults.

Where to see Common in gardens and many other habitats across Britain and much of continental Europe. To see them during the day, turn over logs and stones carefully – that's where they sleep.

What to look for A big blue-black beetle. The legs and antennae are long, and the wing cases and thorax have shiny purple edges. 20–30 mm long.

What they eat A fierce nocturnal hunter that eats slugs and other minibeasts.

Did you know?
Violet Ground Beetles can't fly. They may be called ground beetles, but they will climb up tree trunks when they are hunting.

DEVIL'S COACH HORSE
STAPHYLINUS OLENS

Europe has over 1,000 species of rove beetle – this is one of them. It's long and thin, and about 20–30 mm in length. If it's threatened, its 'tail' goes up like a scorpion's, its massive jaws are opened wide and it lets rip with a smelly chemical from its rear! This beetle can bite – the bite can hurt and it might even bleed.

STAG BEETLE
LUCANUS CERVUS

When to see May to August, particularly on warm evenings.

Where to see Rare in Europe, but can still be seen in some areas of southern Britain. London is a good place to see Stag Beetles! They are found in woods and parks, but many records are now from gardens. They fly well and are attracted to light.

What to look for A big beetle – at 20–75 mm long this is the biggest beetle in Europe. Its head and thorax are black, and the wing cases are brown, although they can be nearly black in the female. The 'antlers' are actually jaws – the males fight with them, but do not normally harm each other. Not all males have big antlers – entomologists once thought that small males with small antlers were a different species, but this is not the case. Females don't have big antlers, but beware – they are the ones that might bite!

What they eat The adults eat sap that leaks out of trees. The larvae eat decaying wood.

Did you know?
Stag Beetles lay their eggs in rotting wood, especially that of oak trees. It can be five years before the adult emerges, but the adult only lives for a few weeks.

7-SPOT LADYBIRD
COCINELLA 7-PUNCTATA

When to see March to October.

Where to see Very common almost anywhere in Britain. Found across much of Europe.

What to look for This is our most familiar ladybird. Look for red wing cases with seven black spots, one of which is shared between the two wing cases. The front end is black, with two obvious pale patches. The markings don't vary much in this species. About 5–8 mm long.

What they eat Adults and larvae eat aphids. Aphids can be a pest so this is a good animal to have in the garden!

7-spot
Ladybird

Did you know?

Handle ladybirds carefully or they will release a foul-smelling chemical onto you! It comes out of their legs and is what their warning colours are warning about.

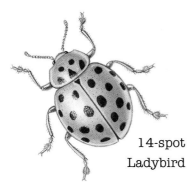

14-spot
Ladybird

14-SPOT LADYBIRD
PROPYLEA QUATUORDECIMPUNCTATA

A common yellow and black ladybird, which is very variable. It can have anywhere between 4 and 14 spots (although mostly it's 14). The spots can be black on a yellow background, or the other way round, and sometimes they join together!

2-SPOT LADYBIRD
ADALIA BIPUNCTATA

The pattern of this common red and black ladybird species is more variable than the 7-spot's. Sometimes, particularly in the north of Britain, the main colour is black rather than red.

BROAD-BODIED CHASER

LIBELLULA DEPRESSA

When to see May to August.

Where to see Common in southern Britain. Likes small sunny ponds. Lives in most of Europe except the far north.

What to look for The 'true' dragonflies are much stouter than damselflies (see below). They rest with their wings open. Most species' eyes are not separated. Mature male Broad-bodied Chasers are mostly blue. Young males and females are mostly yellowish or brown. 39–48 mm long.

What they eat Flying insects.

Did you know?

Young 'BBCs' are sometimes found near woods. Take care – their yellow colouring makes them look a bit like giant wasps or hornets!

BLUE-TAILED DAMSELFLY

ISCHNURA ELEGANS

Damselflies are long, thin delicate insects with separated eyes. At rest, their wings are folded along their abdomen or partly open. Males of this species are dark with a blue 'tail'. Damselflies mate in the 'wheel' position – which looks like a heart shape. The Blue-tailed Damselfly may spend six hours mating. 30–34 mm long.

VELVET MITE
EUTROMBIDIUM ROSTRATUS

When to see Especially in spring.

Where to see Look on walls and garden paths.

What to look for A small, red velvety blob. At 3–4 mm long, this is a big mite! It has eight legs (like spiders), but no waist (unlike spiders).

What they eat A predator that dines on small insects and insect eggs.

Did you know?
You may not have noticed them, but if you have a garden, the chances are that there are millions of mites in it.

HARVESTMAN
PHALANGIUM OPILIO

When to see June to December. Comes out to hunt at night, but can be seen during the day.

Where to see Across Britain and continental Europe.

What to look for Spider-like bug with very long legs and no waist. Does not make webs or venom. About 5–8 mm long.

What they eat Invertebrates, fungi, carrion and bird pooh!

Did you know?
Harvestmen will shed a leg (or several!) to escape a predator. That's fine unless they lose the second pair, the tips of which help them to know where they are going.

GARDEN or CROSS SPIDER
ARANEUS DIADEMATUS

When to see June to November. Especially obvious in autumn.

Where to see Very common in Britain and across continental Europe. Found in gardens, hedges and woods, and on heaths. Almost-circular web can be 40 cm across. Rests close to web during daylight hours, and comes out as it gets dark.

What to look for
A big spider – up to 18 mm long. It has a cross pattern on its abdomen.

What they eat
Flies, wasps, butterflies and other insects.

Did you know?
A single female lays a clump of up to 88 eggs in autumn. She dies about a month later and the eggs hatch in spring.

CRAB SPIDER
XYSTICUS CRISTATUS

When to see April to September.

Where to see Common across Britain and found in most of continental Europe except the far north. Look for it on the ground or lurking in flowers or on other low vegetation.

What to look for A small spider that stands like a crab and moves like one! Females are 6–8 mm long, males 3–5 mm long and with stronger markings than females. Crab spiders wait for their food to come to them, and then leap on it.

What they eat Insects, including aphids.

Did you know?
Unlike most spiders, crab spiders will eat ants.

COMMON WOODLOUSE
ONISCUS ASELLUS

When to see
Especially common if there's wet weather in spring or autumn. They are most active at night.

Where to see Common across Britain and continental Europe. Woodlice, and this species in particular, like damp places. Rotting trees and compost heaps are worth checking for them, or look under logs and stones.

What to look for Its pale edges. There may be pale spots on its back too. This species grows up to 16 mm long. It has 14 legs.

What they eat Diet includes rotting wood, dead and rotting plant material, plants, dead animals, fungi and animal pooh, including their own!

Did you know?
Woodlice aren't insects – they are crustaceans and are related to crabs and lobsters.

PILL WOODLOUSE
ARMADILLIUM VULGARE
About 20 mm long with a glossy grey-black body. The back is obviously dome shaped. It rolls up into a ball, which protects it from predators and drying out. It's also known as the Pill Bug, and yes, people did once take them as medicine!

COMMON CENTIPEDE
LITHOBIUS FORFICATUS

Did you know?
Look at this centipede's legs. They get longer and longer as you move from head to tail. This means that it can run without tripping over its feet!

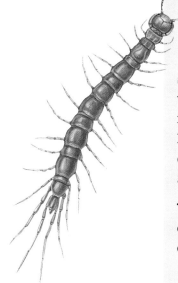

When to see A fierce night-time hunter. You can find it during the day by looking under logs, stones and bark.

Where to see Found across Europe in many habitats, including gardens.

What to look for Flattened, glossy golden-brown body with 7 to 15 pairs of legs and only 1 pair on each segment (millipedes like the one shown below have 2 pairs per segment). It can move very fast (much faster than a millipede). It's carnivorous (unlike millipedes, which are vegetarian), and its speed helps it to catch its animal prey. Antennae enable it to locate prey by smell and touch. 20–30 mm long.

What they eat Invertebrates including beetles and other insects and their larvae, worms, slugs and other centipedes.

COMMON FLAT-BACKED MILLIPEDE
POLYDESMUS ANGUSTUS
This is one of about 50 British millipede species. Compost heaps and under rotting leaves are good places to look for it. Unlike a centipede, it is a slow mover, even though it has up to 74 legs!

Adults have 20 segments, and most of the segments have 2 pairs of legs. 20–25 mm long.

SMOOTH or COMMON NEWT
TRITURUS VULGARIS

When to see Easiest between February and June at breeding ponds, particularly at night.

Where to see Common in much of Britain and found in most of continental Europe. Breeds in small ponds that have a bit of shade, including garden ponds. It is sometimes found under logs.

What to look for A lizard-like amphibian. During the breeding season the male has lots of dark spots and a crest running along almost his entire length and under his tail. His pale belly has a yellow to orange band and dark spots. Breeding season females are 'crestless', with speckles above and small spots underneath – on the throat and maybe on the yellow to orange belly. At other times of the year both male and female are less marked, with smooth brown skin, and the male's crest is much smaller. 60–100 mm long.

What they eat Invertebrates including insects, caterpillars, worms, slugs, snails and water fleas.

Did you know?

Newts spend most of their lives on land. It may be two years or more before a young newt moves to a pond to breed. During their land phase they spend the day under logs, rocks and so on, coming out at night. They hibernate too.

Newts mating – you can easily see the spiked crest on the male's back.

40

COMMON FROG
RANA TEMPORARIA

When to see February to October, especially at night. Hibernates from October under logs or leaves, or in mud at the bottom of a pond.

Where to see Common across Britain and found in much of continental Europe, but not as numerous as it used to be. Garden ponds are now very important for Common Frogs. It also likes damp fields and woods.

What to look for Adults are around 60–80 mm long, sometimes more, with the females larger than the males. Most are green or brown with dark spots, but other colours include yellowish, pink, reddish, grey and black. Some breeding males have a blue gloss on their throats. Their skin is smoother than that of a Common Toad (see below), and the pupil is oval in shape. Frogs hop, while Common Toads normally crawl.

What they eat Invertebrates, especially slugs. Also beetles, flies, caterpillars, worms, spiders, harvestmen and snails.

Did you know?
Common Frogs are a bit like chameleons – they can make their skin paler or darker to improve their camouflage.

COMMON TOAD

BUFO BUFO

Look for this toad in damper parts of the garden. Adults protect themselves from predators by producing a poison in glands behind their eyes. This keeps most animals away. Hedgehogs use it too – they rub their prickles in it for protection!

GRASS SNAKE and VIPER or ADDER
NATRIX NATRIX and VIPERA BERUS

These are the only snake species found in Britain. Of the two, the Viper is much less common in gardens.

When to see Look for the Grass Snake sunbathing on sunny days in summer.

Where to see An excellent swimmer, the Grass Snake is often found near water. It visits gardens to feed, and may lay eggs in open compost heaps – the rotting compost works like an incubator. The Viper is occasionally spotted in very large gardens.

Grass Snake

Did you know?

Vipers are venomous and should be treated with caution, even though they rarely inflict a serious wound. Grass Snakes release a stinky fluid from their back end when alarmed, although their venom has no effect on humans.

What to look for Female Grass Snakes may reach more than 1,800 mm in length. The Viper is up to 600 mm long.

Viper

What they eat Both species eat amphibians, small mammals and birds. The Grass Snake also eats animals that live entirely underwater, such as fish.

SLOW WORM

ANGUIS FRAGILIS

The Slow Worm may look like a snake, but it's actually a lizard with no legs. Up to about 400 mm long, Slow Worms don't lay eggs but produce live young. They eat slugs and snails. One Slow Worm that was kept in captivity lived for 54 years!

EUROPEAN HEDGEHOG

ERINACEUS EUROPAEUS

When to see March to October, especially at night, although sometimes seen in daylight. Hibernates from around October to April in a nest of leaves under thick bushes or logs, or even in garden sheds. Always check winter bonfires for hibernating hedgehogs. May be active on mild winter days.

Where to see Common in mainland Britain and found on most of the Continent. Habitats include gardens, parks, woods and hedgerows.

What to look for It's easy to identify – there's nothing else like it in Britain! It curls up into a spiny ball for protection. It can climb walls and swim. 150–340 mm long, of which about 20 mm is tail.

What they eat Beetles, caterpillars, worms and slugs. Also birds' eggs and small vertebrates, including fish.

Did you know?

Hedgehog spines are customized hairs. One hedgehog has about 5,000 spines – and a really large one could have 7,500. When hedgehogs hibernate, their temperature drops and their pulse rate falls to less than 20 beats a minute. During it's night-time snufflings, a hedgehog's long legs can carry it 1 or 2 km.

COMMON SHREW
SOREX ARANEUS

Did you know?

Scientists estimate that there are around 42 million Common Shrews in Britain. A Common Shrew weighs between 5 and 14 g and has to eat nearly this many grams of food every day. Imagine if you had to eat close to your own weight in food every day!

When to see Any time of year (though less active in winter), and any time of day or night. They can't survive for more than a few hours without eating and so get little rest!

Where to see The second most common mammal in mainland Britain. Found in most of continental Europe, but not Ireland, Portugal and most of France and Spain. Lives in many habitats – woods, hedges and grassy areas are particularly good.

What to look for Normally stays in cover so hard to see alive, but may be glimpsed looking for invertebrates to eat. Often found dead – it releases a horrible-tasting chemical so predators drop it. It is dark brown above and pale underneath with a paler brown band separating the two. The eyes are small, the nose is pointed and the teeth have red tips. The head and body together are 48–80 mm long, and the tail adds another 24–44 mm.

What they eat Invertebrates including beetles and other insects, spiders, woodlice, worms and snails.

RED SQUIRREL
SCIURUS VULGARIS

When to see Any time of year.

Where to see Woods, parks and gardens. The common squirrel in mainland Europe, in the UK it is found only in Scotland, Ireland and a few other areas in the north and south.

What to look for Smaller and more delicate looking than the Grey Squrrel. Prefers to find its food in trees. 180–240 mm long with another 140–200 mm of tail.

What they eat Spruce and pine seeds, acorns, berries, fungi, bark and sap tissue. Special mixes can be bought for garden feeding. Don't just feed them peanuts – try apples and carrots too.

Did you know?

Squirrels bury food just below ground or in tree clefts so that they have food stashed away. They don't remember where the acorns are – but they can smell them! Sadly, Grey Squirrels, introduced to Britain from North America in the 1870s, have driven out native Red Squirrels from many areas. They may also eat birds' eggs and nestlings, which could be making some birds rarer.

GREY SQUIRREL

SCIURUS CAROLINENSIS

The Grey Squirrel is found in woods, parks and gardens in England, Wales and parts of Ireland and Scotland, but not on most of mainland Europe. It can be seen at any time of year, although it is most active in autumn, when it is storing food. It is basically grey above with a brown head, and pale below. When not raiding birdfeeders, it eats seeds including acorns, beechmast and conifer seeds from cones, as well as buds, flowers, fruit and bark.

YELLOW-NECKED MOUSE *APODEMUS FLAVICOLLIS*

When to see Any time of year, but most numerous in autumn. Nocturnal.

Where to see Common in parts of Britain and most of continental Europe. Not found in northern Britain or Ireland. Habitats include woods and hedgerows, and some gardens. Enters houses more often than Wood Mouse.

What to look for It's bigger than a Wood Mouse (see below), with big ears. It is brown above and white underneath, with an obvious divide between the two. The yellow band on its throat is much bigger than that on a Wood Mouse and spreads to the sides. The eyes are large, but not as bulging as those of a Wood Mouse. 95–120 mm long, plus tail of 77–118 mm.

What they eat Seeds, buds, fungi, fruit, insects, worms, snails and centipedes. Sometimes birds' eggs too.

Did you know?

The Yellow-Necked Mouse is an ace climber – it has even been found at the tops of tall trees!

HOUSE MOUSE *MUS MUSCULUS* The mouse that is most often seen in buildings. Small eyes and long tail. 70–100 mm long, plus 65–100 mm of tail.

WOOD MOUSE *APODEMUS SYLVATICUS* Larger than House Mouse. Big bulging eyes, big ears and long tail. There are more of them in Britain than any other rodent species! 81–103 mm long, plus 71–95 mm of tail.

46

BROWN RAT
RATTUS NORVEGICUS

When to see Any time of year, especially from dusk to dawn. Sometimes seen in full daylight.

Where to see Very common in Britain. Often in towns and cities – almost anywhere where there are people. Also farms, sewage farms, rubbish dumps, estuaries, river banks and alongside railway lines. Found across Europe.

What to look for There are lots of them, but they aren't often seen. The Brown Rat looks like a very large mouse. It is brown or greyish-brown above, and lighter below and around the mouth. Sometimes it may be black. The ears are big and the tail is long and scaly. Brown Rats can swim – so don't mistake one for a Water Vole. 130–290 mm long with another 100–200 mm of tail.

What they eat Many things, including seeds, buds, berries, worms, slugs, snails, birds' eggs, dead animals and even cement!

Did you know?
Brown Rats are originally from southern Asia, but have found their way, sometimes by stowing away on boats, to almost everywhere.

RED FOX
VULPES VULPES

When to see Any time of year. Active at night, but also seen around dawn and dusk. May be out during the day when there are cubs to feed.

Where to see Found in most of the northern hemisphere in many habitats – a common visitor to some gardens.

What to look for A dog-like mammal with pointed ears and a bushy tail (called a brush). Most are red-brown above with white around the mouth and on the chest and belly. The brush has a white tip. Males are normally bigger than females. Foxes live in 'earths'. These may be dug by them, or be ex-rabbit burrows or badger setts. Sometimes the space under a garden shed becomes an earth. 620–720 mm long with about 400 mm of tail.

What they eat Small mammals, rabbits, birds, insects, earthworms and dead animals. In towns and cities foxes will scavenge through rubbish. They also like blackberries!

Did you know?
In Britain foxes make a living in towns and cities as well as in the countryside. In the rest of Europe they aren't as common in built-up areas.

Did you know?

A male badger is called a boar. The female is called a sow. A badger sett may be kept in the family and used by several generations of badgers.

When to see Around dusk at any time of year, but less active from November to January. May and June are particularly good. Nocturnal.

Where to see Common across Europe. Setts (the badger's home) are normally in broad-leaved woodland. Badgers may feed in gardens or travel through them – if you're lucky!

What to look for A distinctive sturdy animal with black stripes on its white head, short legs and heavy-duty claws for digging. The setts are underground tunnel systems with multiple entrances, bedrooms and toilets! Tunnels may be 30 m long. Badgers are about 900 mm long.

What they eat Worms, small mammals, insects, moles, rabbits, amphibians, birds' eggs, dead animals, seeds and fruit.

COMMON PIPISTRELLE
PIPISTRELLUS PIPISTRELLUS

When to see April to November, then hibernates. It comes out of roost sites just after sunset.

Where to see Very common in most of Britain. Habitats include gardens, woods, farms and marshy areas. Summer roosts are in buildings, trees and bat boxes. Roosts may be behind boards or tiles, and houses are favourite sites. Found in most of Europe.

What to look for Pipistrelles are the bats most people see, and at 35–45 mm long are Europe's tiniest bats. Their flight twists and turns – helping them catch as many as 3,000 delicious insects every night! They weigh just 3–8 g and have a wingspan of 190–250 mm.

What they eat Small flying insects like midges and moths. Mothers feed young bats on milk.

Did you know?

They really are tiny – you could put one in a matchbox! In 1998 bat experts worked out that what they thought was one species was actually two – the Common Pipistrelle and the Soprano Pipistrelle. 'Sopranos' like wetter places and have a higher frequency call.

BROWN LONG-EARED BAT
PLECOTUS AURITUS
This bat comes out of its roost after dark and hunts for about an hour. Look for the big ears, which can be seen in flight. It catches food in mid-air or plucks it off leaves. It can live for up to 30 years! Its wingspan is 230–285 mm. Grey Long-eared Bats are similar but much rarer.

WOODPIGEON
COLUMBA PALUMBUS

When to see Year round in Britain.

Where to see Found in most of Europe. Nests in trees or bushes on farms, in woods and in towns and cities, including gardens. In gardens feeds on the ground, on bird tables and on ivy.

What to look for A big grey pigeon with a white flash on the neck. In flight, an obvious white crescent is visible across each wing. Listen for the bird's five-part cooing. It may startle you when it flies out of a tree making quite a lot of noise with its wings. 400–420 mm long.

What they eat All sorts of things, but mostly plants like grains, berries, beechmast, beans, clover and cabbage leaves, and potatoes. In gardens eats seeds, bread and other leftovers.

Did you know?
Young Woodpigeons don't have the white neck flash until August or later. This makes them look a bit like the smaller Stock Dove.

COLLARED DOVE
STREPTOPELIA DECAOCTO
Pinky-fawn with darker wingtips, black collar and black tail base. Listen for its three-part cooing. Food includes seeds, elderberries and sometimes invertebrates. In gardens eats leftovers and seeds. Collared Doves arrived in Britain as recently as the 1950s. 310–330 mm long.

BARN SWALLOW
HIRUNDO RUSTICA

When to see April to October in Britain.

Where to see Found in most of Europe. Lives around farms and villages. Nest is built on a beam or something similar, often in barns.

What to look for Blue-black above and mostly whitish below with tail streamers. Brown-red throat with dark band beneath. An aerial insect eater often seen catching food by flying low over water or around cows. It's also seen perched on telephone wires. 170–190 mm long.

What they eat Flying insects.

Did you know?
Swallows are famous migrants, taking on an arduous 9,600-kilometre journey to South Africa every autumn. People once thought they spent winter in mud at the bottoms of ponds!

HOUSE MARTIN
DELICHON URBICA

When to see April to October in Britain.

Where to see Most of Europe.

What to look for Swallow-like bird with forked tail but no streamers. Catches insects in mid-air, sometimes at great heights. Perches on phone wires. Nest is made of mud and secured under eaves on buildings or on cliff faces. 125 mm long.

What they eat Flying insects. Flies and aphids are favourites.

Did you know?
We know that House Martins travel to Africa for the winter, but not that many are seen there – probably because they feed high in the air.

COMMON SWIFT
APUS APUS

When to see In Britain, May to August (sometimes April).

Where to see Most of Europe. Can be seen almost anywhere – in the sky. Nests in older buildings.

What to look for A flying black anchor shape. Listen for it screeching and then look up to find it. 160–170 mm long.

What they eat Flying insects and airborne spiders. Flies and ants are regulars on a Swift's menu.

Did you know?
Swifts are made for the air. They feed in flight, and can sleep and even mate in mid-air. If a Swift finds itself on the ground it's in big trouble – it may not be able to take off.

WREN
TROGLODYTES TROGLODYTES

When to see Year round in Britain.

Where to see The most common bird in Britain. Found in habitats with plenty of undergrowth or bushes.

What to look for Tiny, brown and very active bird with a big voice and short tail. 90–100 mm long.

What they eat Mostly insects and spiders. Loves beetles. Feed it on crumbs.

Did you know?
Male Wrens build a series of nests and the female chooses one of them. In winter Wrens may roost in groups to keep warm. One nest box had 63 Wrens roosting in it!

DUNNOCK
PRUNELLA MODULARIS

When to see In Britain, any time of year.

Where to see Very common across Britain and Ireland, and found in most of continental Europe. Habitats include gardens, woods, bracken and other bushy places.

Adult

What to look for A sparrow-sized bird that's easy to miss! Look for it quietly feeding on the ground, moving like a mouse or singing a gentle musical song from a fairly obvious perch. It looks a bit like a female House Sparrow, but the bill is a very different shape. 145 mm long.

What they eat Insects, and also seeds in winter. In the garden try birdseed, cooked potatoes, fruit, or broken-up cakes or biscuits.

Juvenile

Did you know?
Cuckoos often lay their eggs in Dunnock nests.

Male Dunnocks put on displays, or leks, to attract females.

ROBIN
ERITHACUS RUBECULA

Robins may puff out their feathers in winter to keep warm, making them look much bigger!

When to see In Britain, all year round.

Where to see Found in most of Europe. Habitats include woods, gardens, parks and hedges.

What to look for The Robin is a well-known bird. Roughly sparrow sized, it is brown above and pale below with a dull orange-red breast and face, and a greyish area between the red and brown. Males and females look alike, but young Robins don't have the red breast. 140 mm long.

What they eat Beetles, earwigs, caterpillars and many other bugs, seeds and fruit. They sometimes eat dead animals. More surprising prey includes fish and lizards. Fat and mealworms are garden favourites, although Robins will eat seeds, oats and a range of household leftovers.

Did you know?
Robins sing and defend a territory all year round. In Britain they can be quite tame, but they aren't as tame in the rest of Europe.

BLACKBIRD
TURDUS MERULA

Male

Female

When to see In Britain, all year round.

Where to see Very common in gardens, parks, woods and hedgerows in most of Europe.

What to look for Male is black; female is brown. Look for it on lawns, turning over leaves in flowerbeds or singing a wonderful song from treetops or roofs. 240–250 mm long.

What they eat Earthworms, insects and fruit. In the garden try sultanas, apples or grated cheese.

Did you know?
More than 50 per cent of Blackbirds don't survive their first year. One Blackbird lived for more than 20 years though.

SONG THRUSH
TURDUS PHILOMELOS

Did you know?
Many people think that the Song Thrush's song is one of the best birdsongs. The birds repeat a phrase several times and then move on to another one. Some birds have around 100 phrases to choose from!

When to see Year round in Britain.

Where to see Most of Europe in woods, gardens, parks and hedgerows.

What to look for It is brown above with black spots on its pale underparts. Look for 'anvils' – a concrete path or rock that has been used by the bird to smash open snail shells. 230 mm long.

What they eat Snails, earthworms, caterpillars, beetles and other invertebrates, and fruit. For garden feeding, Blackbird foods should work.

LONG-TAILED TIT
AEGITHALOS CAUDATUS

Look for family parties
of Long-tailed Tits.

Did you know?
In the past, Long-tailed Tits have been
known as Bum Barrels and Bum Towels!

When to see In Britain, any time of year.

Where to see Found in most of Europe. Likes places with trees and bushes, including woods, parks, hedgerows and gardens.

Adult

What to look for A very small bird with a very long tail, often seen in small groups. There is a black stripe over the eye on the side of a whitish head. The body is dark above with a pinkish shoulder patch, and pale underneath with a pinkish flush on the sides and belly. The tail has white edges. Listen for its 'zee-zee-zee' call. It's 140mm long, but 90mm of this is tail!

What they eat Mostly bugs, caterpillars, butterfly and moth eggs, spiders and other invertebrates. Also alder, birch and other seeds. May come to peanut feeders.

Northern
Continental
race (not
normally seen
in Britain)

BLUE TIT
PARUS CAERULEUS

Did you know?

Blue Tit nestlings are fed mostly on caterpillars and they take a lot of feeding. One nest was visited by the parents 1,083 times in just one day.

When to see Year round in Britain.

Where to see Most of Europe in woods, parks and gardens.

What to look for A small bird with a white head with a black stripe through the eye and a blue cap. It's an acrobatic feeder, hanging upside-down if that's what it takes to get at some food. 115 mm long.

What they eat Insects (including caterpillars, flies and beetles), spiders, seeds and fruit. Will take seeds and peanuts from feeders. Also likes cheese, fat and coconut.

GREAT TIT

PARUS MAJOR

At 140 mm long, it's bigger than a Blue Tit. It has a black head with white cheeks, and an obvious black stripe down its belly. It eats lots of different insects, spiders, fruits and seeds. Will take seeds and nuts from feeders, and also likes fat and cheese. Its 'tea-cher' song is well known – but it makes 80 or more other noises too!

MAGPIE
PICA PICA

JAY
GARRULUS GLANDARIUS

When to see Year round in Britain.

Where to see Almost every part of Europe. Often in areas with open ground for feeding, and trees or bushes for nest sites. It is a town and city bird, and a common visitor to gardens.

What to look for Very clever, fairly large bird that is 440–460 mm long, but more than half of this is tail! It makes a loud chattering noise and uses sticks to build a big nest with a roof.

What they eat Insects, carrion, small mammals, eggs, seeds and fruit. They'll take big leftovers from birdtables.

When to see Any time of year.

Where to see Found in most of Europe. Common in woods and areas with older trees.

What to look for Mostly pinky-fawn bird with black moustache and streaky crown feathers (which may be pushed up into a 'crest'). Black-and-white wings with a blue-and-black barred patch, and a black tail. White rump, obvious in flight. 340–350 mm long.

What they eat Invertebrates, small mammals and birds, seeds and fruit. Takes a wide variety of food in gardens, including leftovers.

Did you know?
With the Jay, the Magpie is a member of the Crow family. It has been known to open egg boxes to get at the eggs.

Did you know?
Jays store acorns to help them survive winter. In one wood about 250 Jays were observed carrying off around 3 tonnes of acorns in 20 days!

STARLING
STURNUS VULGARIS

When to see In Britain, all year round.

Where to see Found across most of Europe. Seen in many habitats and often in gardens.

What to look for In summer it is black glossed with green and purple, with a yellow bill. In winter it has lots of spots (mostly whitish below and browner above), and its bill is darker. It is smaller than a Blackbird and has a shorter tail. Also, Starlings walk, while Blackbirds hop. The young are grey-brown. Starlings may feed in gangs on bird tables and lawns. They sing from high points such as trees and TV aerials. The birds form large flocks, especially in winter, sometimes numbering over 100,000 individuals. 215 mm long.

What they eat Many things including bugs (especially insects and insect larvae), fruits and seeds. Will take household scraps, and some take food from feeders.

Adult

Juvenile

Did you know?
Starlings are still common but there are a lot fewer of them than there used to be. They are excellent 'mimics', copying chickens, car alarms, telephones, other wild birds and many other noises.

HOUSE SPARROW
PASSER DOMESTICUS

Male

Did you know?

The number of House Sparrows breeding in Britain has dropped by over 50 per cent in the last 25 years – they are on the UK's Red List of threatened bird species.

Female

Sparrows take dust baths to keep their feathers clean.

When to see In Britain, any time of year.

Where to see Found in most of Europe. Often seen in gardens.

What to look for A smallish bird with a strong, triangular bill. Male is greyish underneath with a black bib, and brown above with black streaks, white wing-bar and grey crown. Female is greyish below and brown with black streaks above. She has no black bib but may have pale 'eyebrows' behind her eyes. 140–150 mm long.

What they eat Mostly seeds, and also berries and shoots. Young are fed mostly on insects. Sparrows will take a wide range of leftovers and food provided for farm animals. They may take seeds and nuts from feeders, and are sometimes seen 'flycatching'. They are also known to steal insects from spiders' webs!

CHAFFINCH
FRINGILLA COELEBS

When to see Year round in Britain.

Where to see Most of Europe, in woods, parks and gardens.

What to look for A sparrow-sized bird. Male is pinky-orange underneath with white wing-bars and outer tail feathers. Female is less colourful. 145 mm long.

What they eat Seeds and invertebrates like caterpillars and beetles. In gardens they will eat seeds and leftovers.

Did you know?
Chaffinches are more common than many people think – there are more breeding in the UK than any other bird species apart from the Wren!

GOLDFINCH
CARDUELIS CARDUELIS

Did you know?
Most of the Goldfinches that breed in Britain don't spend the winter here – they migrate to other parts of Europe. Many end up in France or Spain.

When to see Year round in Britain.

Where to see Found in most of Europe. Habitats include woods, parks and gardens.

What to look for A smallish, very brightly coloured finch. Adult has a distinctive black-and-white head with a red face. 120 mm long.

What they eat Mostly seeds. In gardens they take seeds from feeders. Get a nyjer seed feeder if you want to attract them.

GREENFINCH
CARDUELIS CHLORIS

When to see In Britain, all year round.

Where to see Found in most of Europe. Likes tall trees in gardens, parks, woods and hedgerows. Also feeds on farmland and around the coast in winter.

What to look for A bulky, sparrow-sized finch. Male is mostly green or greeny-yellow. Female is much duller, with yellow in the wings and tail, but not as much as the male. 150 mm long.

What they eat Many different seeds and some invertebrates. In gardens will take seeds and peanuts from feeders. Sunflower seeds are good for attracting Greenfinches.

Did you know?
Humans have introduced Greenfinches to South America, Australia and New Zealand, places where they wouldn't normally live.

SISKIN
CARDUELIS SPINUS

A Goldfinch-sized acrobatic feeder. Male is mostly yellowy green. Female is duller. Spruce, pine, birch and alder seeds are favourite foods. Feeds on nuts and nyjer seed in gardens, and is particularly keen on peanuts in red-netting bags! 120 mm long.

SPOTTED!

You can use the boxes opposite the animal names on this page to tick of the species that you have spotted.

Common Earthworm	❑	Garden Bumblebee ❑	Common Pipistrelle ❑
Garden Snail	❑	Cuckoo Bee ❑	Brown Long-eared Bat ❑
Large Black Slug	❑	Violet Ground Beetle ❑	Woodpigeon ❑
Common Field		Devil's Coach Horse ❑	Collared Dove ❑
Grasshopper	❑	Stag Beetle ❑	Barn Swallow ❑
Oak Bush Cricket	❑	7-spot Ladybird ❑	House Martin ❑
House Cricket	❑	14-spot Ladybird ❑	Common Swift ❑
Common Earwig	❑	2-spot Ladybird ❑	Wren ❑
Common Green		Broad-bodied Chaser ❑	Dunnock ❑
Shield Bug	❑	Blue-tailed Damselfly ❑	Robin ❑
Common Pond Skater	❑	Velvet Mite ❑	Blackbird ❑
Common Froghopper	❑	Harvestman ❑	Song Thrush ❑
Green Lacewing	❑	Garden Spider ❑	Long-tailed Tit ❑
Small White	❑	Crab Spider ❑	Blue Tit ❑
Large White	❑	Common Wooodlouse ❑	Great Tit ❑
Green-veined White	❑	Pill Woodlouse ❑	Magpie ❑
Peacock	❑	Common Centipede ❑	Jay ❑
Red Admiral	❑	Common Flat-backed	Starling ❑
Small Tortoiseshell	❑	Millipede ❑	House Sparrow ❑
Small Magpie	❑	Smooth Newt ❑	Chaffinch ❑
Silver Y	❑	Common Frog ❑	Goldfinch ❑
Large Yellow		Common Toad ❑	Greenfinch ❑
Underwing	❑	Grass Snake ❑	Siskin ❑
Garden Tiger	❑	Slow Worm ❑	
Common Crane Fly	❑	European Hedgehog ❑	
Bluebottle	❑	Common Shrew ❑	
Hoverfly	❑	Grey Squirrel ❑	
Small Black Ant	❑	Red Squirrel ❑	
Red Ant	❑	Yellow-necked Mouse ❑	
Horntail	❑	House Mouse ❑	
Ichneumon Fly	❑	Wood Mouse ❑	
Common Wasp	❑	Brown Rat ❑	
German Wasp	❑	Red Fox ❑	
Honey Bee	❑	Badger ❑	